To:

From:

"If you feel that your company is falling behind with selling and growing as more people move 'online,' then this one-hour read will be the best business investment you make in 2021."

—*Hube Hopkins, President,*
WSI B2B Marketing

"Selling has changed! There's no one better than John Asher to tell you what's working now—the very latest best practices—and what your team needs to do to ensure success in the future."

—*Judy Schramm, CEO, ProResource, Inc.*

THE
FUTURE
OF SALES

The 50+
Techniques, Tools, and Processes
Used by Elite Salespeople

JOHN ASHER

Award-winning author of *Close Deals Faster*

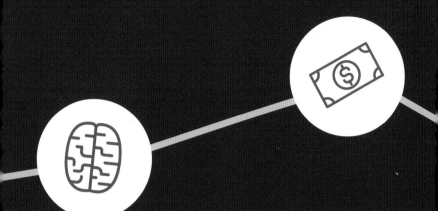

Copyright © 2022 by John Asher
Cover and internal design © 2022 by Sourcebooks
Cover design by Jackie Cummings
Cover images © macrovector/Freepik, Adrien Coquet/Noun Project, Gregor Cresnar/Noun Project, Jacopo Bonacci/Noun Project
Internal images © endsheets, cnythzl/Getty Images; page vi, gpointstudio/Getty Images; page 6, svetikd/Getty Images; page 10, dowell/Getty Images; page 20, Samuel Sanchez/Getty Images; page 27, milanvirijevic/Getty Images; pages 32, 37, Hiraman/Getty Images; pages 46, 69, Westend61/Getty Images; page 51, anyaberkut/Getty Images; page 56, mangpor_2004/Getty Images; page 61, Yuri_Arcurs/Getty Images; page 64, Moyo Studio/Getty Images; page 74, Luis Alvarez/Getty Images; page 79, Oscar Wong/Getty Images; page 84, PixelsEffect/Getty Images

Published by Simple Truths, an imprint of Sourcebooks
P.O. Box 4410, Naperville, Illinois 60567-4410
(630) 961-3900
sourcebooks.com

Printed and bound in the United States of America.
VP 10 9 8 7 6 5 4 3 2 1

This work is dedicated to
THE ASHER SALES TEAM
who work with our prospects and
clients to close deals faster.

TABLE OF CONTENTS

INTRODUCTION

For the past several generations or so, there have been three types of sales:

1 Sales to consumers

2 Sales to business buyers

3 Sales to government buyers

We have all witnessed the fairly quick migration of purchases by consumers from brick-and-mortar to the internet for the past several decades. In 2020, world-wide retail e-commerce sales for the year grew 28 per-cent to $4.3 trillion.[i]

Companies following this trend are more heav-ily investing in digital selling. According to Statista, worldwide digital advertising will grow from $40 billion in 2021 to $46 billion by 2024.[ii] Automation has seen similar growth to support factories and consumers. In early 2020, a Black & Decker factory making portable electrical tools opened in South Carolina. The factory is 100 percent automated. This rise in automation has impacted retail too. Consumers can order, pay for, and have a pizza delivered from Domino's with no clicks. Not one click! If they have their favorite pizza in their Domino's app, just opening the app is enough to order, pay for, and have the pizza delivered.

Every recession results in rapid innovation and many new business start-ups. McKinsey & Company examined supply and demand factors across seven countries and six sectors looking at stalled productivity growth since the 1960s. This period includes all of the factors and setbacks associated with financial crises, armed conflicts, oil disruptions, and market collapses. Their analysis indicates that companies that rapidly innovated new products, services, and processes had the best opportunities to survive and contribute to the return of economic growth through productivity. Looking forward, McKinsey forecasts that "60 percent of the productivity potential comes from digital opportunities."[iii]

One of the most important lessons learned is that the companies that rapidly innovated new products, services, and/or processes grew four times faster from the end of the recession to the start of the next one, usually about ten years. The laggard companies did not innovate, and if they did, they got to the market too late.

The behavior of business buyers has radically

and dramatically changed. Most buyers like the changes. Most elite salespeople and their companies have understood these changes and have rapidly responded to stay ahead of their competitors. You can too!

Our team has identified the sales techniques, processes, and tools that salespeople need to use to adapt or get left behind in the dust! Whether your company works B2B (business to business), B2G (business to government), or standard B2C (business to consumer), sales success in the ever-shifting future will be found only through adaptation. It's time to shake things up!

Radical and Permanent Changes in Buyer Behavior

Most buyers now have a preference for digital interactions with companies and their salespeople. Face-to-face (F2F) interactions have fallen out of favor for a number of readily apparent reasons.

- *The purchase can be accomplished much more quickly and easily.*
- *There will be a digital record of the entire transaction.*
- *It is more efficient.*

- *There are many untrained salespeople who do not have the standard sales skills.*
- *There are some salespeople who are not likable.*
- *Some salespeople have the opposite personality style from the buyer and do not know how to mirror the buyer's style.*
- *There are no delays because of the need for out-of-town travel.*
- *Traffic jams can cause salespeople to be late to meetings.*

As they become more comfortable with the technology, buyers are more frequently using mobile apps to make purchases. According to *Forbes*, the mobile payment market in the United States alone is exceeding $130 billion.[iv] As buyers buy more products online, they are finding opportunities to stay in virtual channels. For example, 43 percent of global shoppers are now doing product research via social networks prior to purchase, before talking with sales representatives.[v] This is ultimately why buyers also expect their online purchases to be simple, safe, secure, and easy to navigate.

Large-scale surveys support observations that buyer behavior has changed in interactions with salespeople. The LinkedIn State of Sales Report 2020 with data from ten thousand online surveys of salespeople shows:

▸ *Virtual selling is going mainstream: 77 percent of respondents are holding more virtual meetings.*

▸ *Buyers are less responsive: 44 percent of respondents anticipated a decrease in responsiveness to outreach.*

▸ *Sales cycles are longer: 44 percent of respondents said buyers' sales cycles increased.[vi]*

▸ *Their responses to unsolicited emails are down by 30 percent.*

▸ *Four out of five buyers prefer to have a video-conferencing meeting, for example through Zoom, than a phone call.*

▸ *Three out of four believe that digital selling is more effective than F2F selling.*

Many B2B buyers have challenges that are now different because of the COVID-19 pandemic and post-pandemic recovery considerations. In addition, many of their customers are also facing new challenges. Because of these new and changing circumstances, buyers expect salespeople to be able to provide deep insights into their business. Many buyers know they need to change, but they do not have the knowledge to be able to do so quickly, efficiently, and with a significant return on their investment.

Buyers are looking for intelligent salespeople who have done their homework and who can challenge them to think differently and guide them through their change journey. In normal times, buyers can evaluate sellers in F2F meetings or at sporting events or business meals. When they are unable or choose not to do so, the next best and most helpful process is to use referrals from others they trust. Referrals have always been important, and now they are more important than ever.

According to Gartner Research, 80 percent of B2B

sales interactions between suppliers and buyers will occur in digital channels by 2025.[vii] In most cases, the first interaction between a prospect and your company will be digital. The significance of this shift is clear. Seventy-five percent of buyers no longer see the value of interacting in-person with salespeople. My company's research and discussions with B2B sales leaders show the following:

- *Buyers want an automated demo in lieu of a demo by a sales rep. There are several reasons for this shift. Many sales reps are not properly trained and keep asking unnecessary questions to get the buyer to say yes.*
- *Sales reps spend too much time selling and not enough time providing key information to help the buyer understand the product. Buyers would actually like a choice of an automated demo, a demo by a sales rep, or an automated demo with the sales rep observing with them.*

▸ *Buyers are also getting used to the use of virtual reality and augmented reality in their personal lives and want to see them used in business demos. Examples include the use of virtual reality in decorating spaces (e.g., Wayfair) and the use of augmented reality in fashion choices (observing the clothing item from every angle).*

Based on LinkedIn research, sales efforts are shifting more toward digital selling to meet current changes in buyer behavior. Closing deals now requires more effort as follows:

▸ *57 percent of sellers are making more phone calls.*

▸ *51 percent of sellers are sending more emails.*

▸ *40 percent of sellers are leveraging more warm outreach.[viii]*

Furthermore, increased remote work for everyone is here to stay. PWC's Remote Work Survey reveals:

▸ *83 percent of employers now say the shift to remote work has been successful*

▸ *Less than 20 percent of executives say they want to return as many of their people to the office as they had pre-pandemic*

▸ *61 percent of employees expect to spend only half their future time in the office[ix]*

A transformation in sales strategies, sales processes, and resource allocation is needed. Companies will need to shift from being seller-centric to being buyer-centric and from analog to hyperautomated.

Forrester Research found in 2017 that one in five buyers did not want to meet with a sales rep in person. Their 2020 analysis shows that number has increased to more than one in three.[x] This means that while some deals may still be closed F2F, most initial engagements will start with marketing. More often than not, sales reps will engage only near the end of the buyer's journey. Pre-pandemic, the buyer's journey was approximately

70 percent complete before they interacted with a salesperson. Post-pandemic it is closer to 90 percent.

Finally, nearly three out of four B2B buyers are now millennials or younger. They expect the B2B purchasing process to have the same kind of speed and ease of use as the B2C process. Baby boomer–style white papers are giving way to value-adding video content.[xi] Companies will therefore need to build digital buyer experiences to support buyers in their self-learning and their change journey.

In addition to these buyer trends, it is apparent that there will be large changes for salespeople from outside to inside sales, from F2F to digital interactions, and from field sales and account managers to virtual sales. And a much smaller number of salespeople will be needed. These trends illustrate why the advanced tools, techniques, and processes described in this book are so important for ensuring that you are one of the remaining elite salespeople in the future.

CHAPTER

TWO

Advanced Prospecting Technology

The percentage of buyers who want an F2F meetup with a salesperson has significantly decreased. The importance of the digital presence of salespeople has therefore increased proportionally.

Most buyers valued F2F meetings with salespeople so they could size them up from personal and professional standpoints. Most buyers want to assess the personal attributes of salespeople, such as honesty, integrity, and likability. Appearance is also important to buyers.

The best way for a salesperson to gain a buyer's trust is with a strong referral from someone the buyer already trusts. The importance of referrals has increased significantly. If you ask most salespeople for the best source of referrals, most of them will respond "our best customers." Wrong! Current customers are the second-best source of referrals.

The best sources of referrals are your company vendors, suppliers, subcontractors, advisors, and consultants. Why? Because your company is paying them. If you ask them for referrals, are they going to blow you off? No, because they want to keep your business. In most cases, they want to increase it. When you ask, most of them will provide a referral.

Once you are given the referral, you need to play detective. Start asking questions to determine important information about the referral, such as their need for your products or services, their contact information, and the company's buying processes. Are they a qualified buyer? If your source has positive responses to all your questions, ask them to set up an initial virtual call for the three of you.

Elite salespeople and their companies are known as "thought leaders." Thought leadership content is authoritative, of superior quality, consistent, comprehensive, and most of all useful to the recipient. LinkedIn research shows that 92 percent of buyers are willing to engage with professionals who are known industry thought leaders, as they can provide expert guidance.[xii] Buyers will also respond to sellers who saw the buyers' social media post and responded with either a link to a relevant third-party thought leadership post or their company's relevant thought leadership content.

Since so many interactions with buyers are not in F2F meetings, sales reps need to perform more thorough research on buyers, their company, and their company's competitors. Industry association websites and Dun & Bradstreet can be useful for this research. Here is a list of information to look for:

1. Research your prospect's company to assess their company history and management team.

2. Research your prospect's offerings; what solutions do they provide for their customers?

3. Research your prospect's industry; what challenges are emerging in their industry?

4. Research your prospect's competition; where is your prospect positioned in the marketplace? And can you help them?

5. Research your prospect's challenges and aspirations. Here are four sources elite salespeople use: The person who gave them the prospect referral; their "inside coach"; research on their industry; and research on their company and their company's competitors.

The best way to research buyers themselves is with LinkedIn, specifically with Sales Navigator (see Chapter 6). Of all the social media networks, it is almost always the most reliable as the information is provided by the buyers themselves and it is mainly business related. It can also provide salespeople with information they can use to build rapport.

LinkedIn and Sales Navigator have become so important to hunter salespeople because, even during the pandemic, 80 percent of B2B leads from social networks come from them.[xiii] Here are ten LinkedIn metrics that matter (note that LinkedIn changes the limits and requirements frequently):

1 Total number of connections.

2 100 percent complete profile.

3 Profile-oriented to educate prospects about your value proposition.

4 Number of connection requests (three hundred characters max) sent per week (max one hundred).

5 Number of prospects who looked at your profile when sent a connection request.

6 Percentage of connection requests accepted.

7 Number of prospects accepting the connection request and actively engaging.

8 Number of relevant quality messages sent.

9 Response rate to InMail posts (sales introduction messages) (max fifteen per month).

10 Number of people viewing your Thought Leadership posts.

Before reaching out, you can use resources such

as Crystal Knows (discussed further in Chapter 6) to determine the buyer's personality type. Sales reps can tailor their emails, voicemails, and discussions to the buyer's exact personality type.

To entice a buyer to connect on LinkedIn, let them know what value you can bring to them. Examples are as follows:

- *You understand their needs and have options to share.*
- *You have researched their customers and have some insight to share.*
- *You have recently helped other companies in their industry increase their revenue/profitability/efficiency*

Here is how low-performing salespeople reach out. Their message is all about their offering. Not only does it not work, it is irritating to most buyers: "*I would like to add you to my professional network and show you how our new app will improve the operations efficiency of your facilities team.*"

A much better way to send a post to a prospect would be to replace "I" with "you" to activate the buyer's brain with information about them. Make it focused on the buyer.

"From researching your website, I can see that you are continually searching for new innovative tools to offer your customers. Our customers have been benefiting from our app that improves their efficiency by 17 percent or more. If you are interested in viewing a quick demo, let's connect, and I'll set it up for you and/or your team to review."

Once the buyer has expressed an interest by connecting, propose a virtual meeting (e.g., Zoom). LinkedIn studies show that these interactions are much more welcome than a phone call for three fourths of the buyers. The buyer can now size you up from a visual standpoint. Both buyer and seller can be expressive and both can observe eye contact and read facial expressions and body language. Buyers will stay in a Zoom meeting longer than a phone call. Deals are much more likely to close in a virtual meeting than a phone call.

Once they have agreed to virtual meetings or phone calls, you are ready to apply the advanced sales process elite salespeople use to go from the start of the meetup to closing a new deal or closing the next step to a new deal.

The process has three simple steps:

▸ **Step One:** *Build rapport and trust (Chapter 3).*

▸ **Step Two:** *Perform a brilliant needs analysis to find out exactly what the buyer needs by being a great listener. Then offer a solution that provides a rationale to help the buyer complete their change journey. In some cases, you'll need to gain buyer acceptance by giving them a demo, and in some cases, you may need to differentiate your company's offerings (Chapter 4).*

▸ **Step Three:** *Close the deal or the next step in the buyer's journey (Chapter 5).*

Two Advanced Techniques to Build Rapport and Trust

Action selling teaches us that all buyers make five decisions about a salesperson, their offerings, and the company they represent—in the following order:

1 They have to buy you!

2 They have to buy your organization as credible and having a good reputation.

3 They have to buy your offerings as able to help them with their challenge.

4 They have to buy the price of your offerings.

5 They have to decide when to buy.

If they do not buy the salesperson, the buyer will not continue the journey though the other four steps.

We are all social beings. All of us thrive on interactions with other people, some more than others. So this becomes the most important step.

There are a number of actions salespeople can take to build a relationship with the buyer. Most of the techniques are based on solid neuroscience principles called cognitive biases. These biases have been developed by the emotional and rational portions of the brain to keep us safe. They are shortcuts, rules of thumb, and tendencies that almost always give us the right answer quickly.

Here are a few important biases that apply to rapport building for you to explore and use to your advantage.

Similarity Bias

When we meet people who are not similar to us, our brains raise a warning flag. We like people who are like us in dress, looks, and interests. We are more likely to buy from salespeople who are similar in age, religion, political leanings, and sports preferences.

This chart shows the four classic personality styles. Matching the buyer's style signals the buyer's brain that we are similar to them and safe.

The Four Personality Types

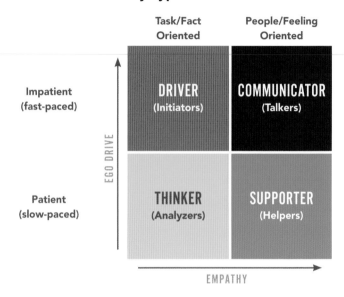

Other techniques include using neurolinguistic pro-gramming to appear similar by matching:

- *Speed of talking*

- *Volume of speech*

- *Body language*

- *Using acronyms used by the buyer*

- *Breathing rates*

When we use these techniques to appear similar to the buyer, their decision-making brain signals to their rational brain, "Wow! This person is just like me. Therefore, they must be great!"

Compliment Bias

This is a simple one with which to strategize. We are biased toward people who compliment us. When we compliment the buyer, it can be about them, their product, their website, their spaces, or their company. Compliments should be authentic, meaningful, sincere, and specific.

Reciprocity Bias

We are biased toward people who give us something. Our brains are biased to return the gift. "Much obliged" is a saying that illustrates the point. Always give the buyer a gift. Bring them a book relevant to their job or their industry. Send them relevant articles.

Once you have met, continue your gifts in all interactions that you can. Gifts don't have to be material. If you give the buyer the gift of really listening to their needs, they will immediately return the gift by providing insights into their needs. The next gift they will give you is listening intently to your offer to help. The details of how to give the gift of listening are described in the next chapter. Roger Staubach, Hall of Fame quarterback and very successful business leader, has only one mantra for his people: "There are no traffic jams on the extra mile." It means if you do extra for your customers and prospects, you separate yourself from most other salespeople.

Lastly, find out the background of the buyer from networking and social media websites. LinkedIn is a useful one for business. When you find out more about their background, you can almost always find similarities that can be used in rapport building. I was once referred to a CEO by a friend. In researching his

background on LinkedIn, I found the following similarities between us:

- *CEO*
- *Global company*
- *MBA*
- *Engineer*
- *Soccer*
- *Baseball*
- *Author*
- *Three daughters*
- *German language*
- *Belgian beer*
- *Outgoing personality style*
- *Vistage (CEO group) member*

In business settings, it is usually best to start rapport building with business, technical, or professional similarities, so I chose our shared Vistage involvement, leading to a long conversation, great rapport, and a lifetime global customer.

Building trust with a buyer is also important. However, feeling comfortable with the other person is only one of the six factors used to develop trust. Here are the basic four:

1 **Likability:** A feeling of similarities and understanding.

2 **Honesty:** We all want to deal with honest people.

3 **Integrity:** People who will do what they say they will do, the way it should be done, and on time. And if they cannot, then they will alert us, take responsibility for the mess they have created for us, and let us know when they will get it done.

4 **Product knowledge:** It is great when salespeople have great personality characteristics and we like them, but it is not enough for us to trust them as a salesperson. They must have strong product knowledge so we know they can help us.

In the post-pandemic era, there are two additional factors that buyers need to trust a salesperson:

5 Salespeople must be totally proficient in the use of the virtual conferencing platforms (e.g., Zoom). They must know how to do the following basics in the virtual landscape:

- Set up a meeting
- Get the time zone right
- Be able to manipulate the system
- Be familiar with the technology
- Know how to display a document like a proposal
- Know how to modify the proposal in real time
- Have the ability to have the buyer sign the proposal (if appropriate in real time electronically)

6 As previously mentioned, the use of LinkedIn has skyrocketed during the pandemic. There are now over 700 million users worldwide. When a salesperson reaches out to a buyer though LinkedIn, the buyer will consider responding. Before they do, they will look at the salesperson's LinkedIn profile. If it is not completely up-to-date or it is oriented to helping that salesperson find another sales position, in the vast majority of cases, the buyer will not connect. Therefore, having a complete and current LinkedIn profile is an important element in the buyer's decision process of trusting a salesperson.

Now that we have built rapport and trust with the buyer, when they determine they are ready to shift to a business discussion, we can shift to **Step Two** (see page 19), performing a needs analysis and offering a compelling solution.

CHAPTER

FOUR

Performing a Needs Analysis and Offering a Compelling Solution

Buyers always appreciate interacting with salespeople who put the buyer first. The top salespeople understand this desire and they put the buyers' needs before their quota using a five-step process:

1 Learn by listening first: "Perfect" listening is critical to the buyer-seller relationship.

2 Share readily: Empower buyers with robust information and transparency.

3 Solve, don't sell: Make your main success "problems solved."

4 Deliver continuing value: Build the relationship after a deal is signed.

5 Earn and keep trust: Always act in the buyer's best interest and earn the title of "trusted advisor."

When rapport building has been successful, the buyer will signal when it is time to shift the conversation to business. That signal usually indicates they are now comfortable with you.

The buyer will then usually ask the salesperson to describe their offerings with questions such as the following:

▸ *Tell me about your products.*

▸ *Tell me about your company.*

▸ *How can you help us?*

At this point, the average salesperson will start talking about their offerings, in many cases starting with a presentation. This is the easy path for salespeople. They have given many of these presentations and are comfortable doing so. But it is not the most effective path. Elite salespeople know that a much better path is to engage the buyer to start talking about their current challenges (fix a problem) or an aspiration (improvement).

They will get the buyer talking by saying, "*I'm prepared to discuss our many options, but if I could ask you a couple of questions first, we can narrow our discussion to provide options to best fit your needs. Would that be okay?*"

An example of a customer challenge would be that they are concerned about cybersecurity threats.

To get the buyer to talk first, the salesperson could say, "*I would be happy to show you our seven different cybersecurity solutions. It might save us some time if you could start by describing your biggest concerns in this area.*"

An example of a customer aspiration might be that they want faster growth rates and more consistent profitability. To get the buyer to talk first, the salesperson could say, "*We have many techniques to help companies grow faster with more consistent profitability. If you could start by giving a quick history of the company's growth over the past several years, I will be able to show you which strategies would fit your needs.*"

A key point in neuroscience is that buyers value what they say more than what a salesperson says to them. So after describing their needs, they feel good.

An even better methodology is to describe your research (see Chapter 2) and start with your knowledge of their challenges or aspirations. An example might be as follows:

Here is my understanding of your main challenges: Your salespeople are having difficulty finding prospects. Once they find likely prospects for your collaboration software, their conversion rate to a qualified lead is too low. Once they have an initial conversation with the prospect, their closing rates are too low.

Do I have these concerns about right?

Now you have signaled to the buyer you are in the elite salesperson category. You have performed brilliant research. You do not have to be a "solution" seller who starts by asking questions to discover needs. Your research has taken you much further down the path to understanding what the buyer needs and being prepared to offer appropriate solutions.

Based on our experience with eighty thousand salespeople and their interactions with buyers, your research and your question about having the buyer's concerns right will result in the buyer talking about their needs 95 percent of the time. Once the discussion about the details of their needs is complete, elite salespeople can select just the necessary slides from their presentation slide deck to discuss with the buyer because they are the few that totally relate to the buyer's needs. Now it is obvious how you can devise a solution to the buyers' challenge or aspiration.

Once the buyer starts talking about their needs, the average salesperson will passively listen. This technique means they will listen just enough to recognize a need and start offering solutions, often interrupting the buyer. This technique is a turnoff to most buyers. They will consider these salespeople to have "commission breath," meaning they know the seller is just after a quick commission.

Elite salespeople have always practiced a different form of listening called active listening. The active listener will keep on asking questions until they fully understand the customer's needs. Ninety percent will take notes as the buyer is talking. These elite salespeople know there are eight benefits, most based on neuroscience studies, to taking notes:

1 It only takes 20 percent of your brain to listen. If you are not taking notes, it is difficult to stay focused on the buyer. It is easy for your mind to get distracted. Listening, processing what the buyer is saying, and taking notes takes 80 percent of your brain. Now it is much easier to stay engaged and focused on what the buyer is saying.

2 It communicates that you are actively listening.

3 It causes buyers to take you more seriously.

4 It relieves buyers' anxiety.

5 It increases retention by 40–70 percent.

6 You can only remember three main points when not taking notes.

7 It slows down the needs analysis, giving the buyer more time to provide more information. And it gives more time to think of follow-up questions.

8 It provides information to enter into your customer relationship management (CRM) system.

Most salespeople are pretty faithful about using this technique. Elite salespeople add two more steps: they ask permission to take notes prior to doing so, and when they have completed their notes, they summarize and repeat the buyer's points back to them to ensure they have them right. Let's look at the details.

Elite salespeople not only take notes but start by asking permission to take them. There are five great reasons to do so:

1 Buyers do not want to waste time on salespeople who do not take notes, offer solutions that are not right, and totally waste the buyer's time. Buyers want you to get it right! Therefore, 100 percent of buyers will agree to let you take notes.

2 It is polite and shows respect.

3 It gives control (or the illusion of control) of the conversation to the buyer. But since you're asking the questions and guiding the conversation where you need it to go to determine the buyers' needs, you are actually in control of the conversation.

4 It lets skeptical buyers know exactly what you are doing. Some could be worried that you are doodling.

5 You get the first yes in the staircase to the yes to closing the deal you want. As you go through the buyer's purchasing process, you may have to close several steps. You want a yes for them to agree to your proposed next step, such as agreeing to a demo.

After performing this step, the buyer's comfort level is now at 75 percent, which is very comfortable with a stranger. Unfortunately, only 10 percent of salespeople ask permission to take notes and miss out on these five very useful benefits.

Elite salespeople repeat back what they have heard to the buyer to verify that they have understood what the buyer has told them. Unfortunately, only 2 percent of salespeople execute this technique. Here are the incredible reasons for doing so:

1 Your summary results in one of two outcomes:

- You have it exactly right, which has a great and positive impact on the buyer.
- You do not have it exactly right, allowing the buyer to correct you and preventing you from making a big mistake by offering a solution that does not fit the buyer's needs.

2 The buyer's comfort level rises to 85 percent.

3 The buyer wants you to get the business, or if it is a bigger opportunity, they want you to submit a very competent and price competitive proposal.

4 The buyer will give you the information they know you need to get the business, including the following:

- Information they forgot to tell you
- Priority of their requirements/specs
- Information about the incumbent
- Information about your competition
- Information about internal politics
- Their company's decision-making process
- The personality types of other buyers
- Their time frame
- Their budget (60 percent of the time)
- The potential for increased scope of work

To reiterate the percentage of salespeople performing at the highest level when asking questions and listening during a needs analysis is as follows.

Ninety percent take notes. Only 10 percent ask permission to take notes. Only two percent summarize the buyer's points back to the buyer as many times as it takes to get agreement from the buyer that they have it exactly right.

As a final note, if elite salespeople do not have a solution that fits the buyer's needs, they will go find the right solution provider. Once these elite salespeople do this for buyers, they become trusted advisors for life! The buyer knows that whatever change journeys they have in the future will be facilitated brilliantly by their trusted advisor.

In the next chapter, you will learn how elite salespeople differentiate themselves and close the deal.

CHAPTER

FIVE

Advanced Techniques to Differentiate and Close the Sale

As you approach the ability to close a sale, you may need to differentiate your offerings and/or your company to give the buyer the confidence that they are making the correct choice. There are three standard ways to differentiate and a new one based on the virtual selling world we are now in.

The first and most powerful way to differentiate is to have a unique selling proposition. The neuroscience behind this concept is that one of the principal ways to activate the buyer's decision-making brain is with a clear distinction. The brain makes quick "no" decisions about similar (boring) patterns. It likes what is new better than what is improved. The brain loves bright, shiny, stark differences.

Here is a bad example: "*We have been in business for thirty-five years! We have great customer service. We have a strong engineering team.*" The buyer hears "Blah, blah, blah," and the decision-making brain says no.

Here is a good example: "*We are the only global sales training company where every trainer is a former CEO of a company.*" In this statement, the word *only* shows the uniqueness of the company and wakes up the buyer's brain.

Here is an example of the power of having a unique selling proposition. Your company and two others are in competition for a new opportunity with a buyer. In the buyer's mind, all three companies, including yours, have good experience, a stellar reputation, good quality, good service, and reasonable prices. The buyer considers all three companies tied for first and has a difficult time deciding. Where does the discussion almost always go? The price. Competition based solely on the low price is not a position that salespeople want to find themselves in.

On the other hand, if one of the companies is clearly better, as they have a strong, unique selling proposition, the buyer will make a quick decision, and the price usually never comes up. And the buyer considers the decision to be risk-free.

Another way to differentiate a company is to have a strong WHY (sometimes called a company purpose).

One of the highest rated TED Talks ever is Simon Sinek's "Start with Why." As Sinek says, "Every company can describe what they do. Every company can describe how they do what they do. Very few companies can describe why they do what they do."

If your company has a compelling WHY that connects with employees, customers, and prospects, you are on a great path to differentiation in the buyer's mind.

Here is an example. We have a customer who owns a very successful pest control services company. Now you may think this company is selling a commodity. Okay, they are going to come over and spray for bugs. Lots of companies can do this, so why not select the company with the lowest prices?

This company's WHY is "to save the planet." Their WHY drives them to use nontoxic chemicals whenever possible and to emphasize green technologies whenever they can. When you survey consumers and ask them about this company's WHY 85 percent like it. Most like it a lot. Their WHY does a great job of differentiating their company. They are the fastest-growing pest control service company in their metropolitan area.

A third way to differentiate is to have strong, relevant case studies of how your company has helped other companies similar to the prospect company (e.g., in the same or similar industry). These stories are another way to wake up the buyer's decision-making brain. The importance of stories is based on human

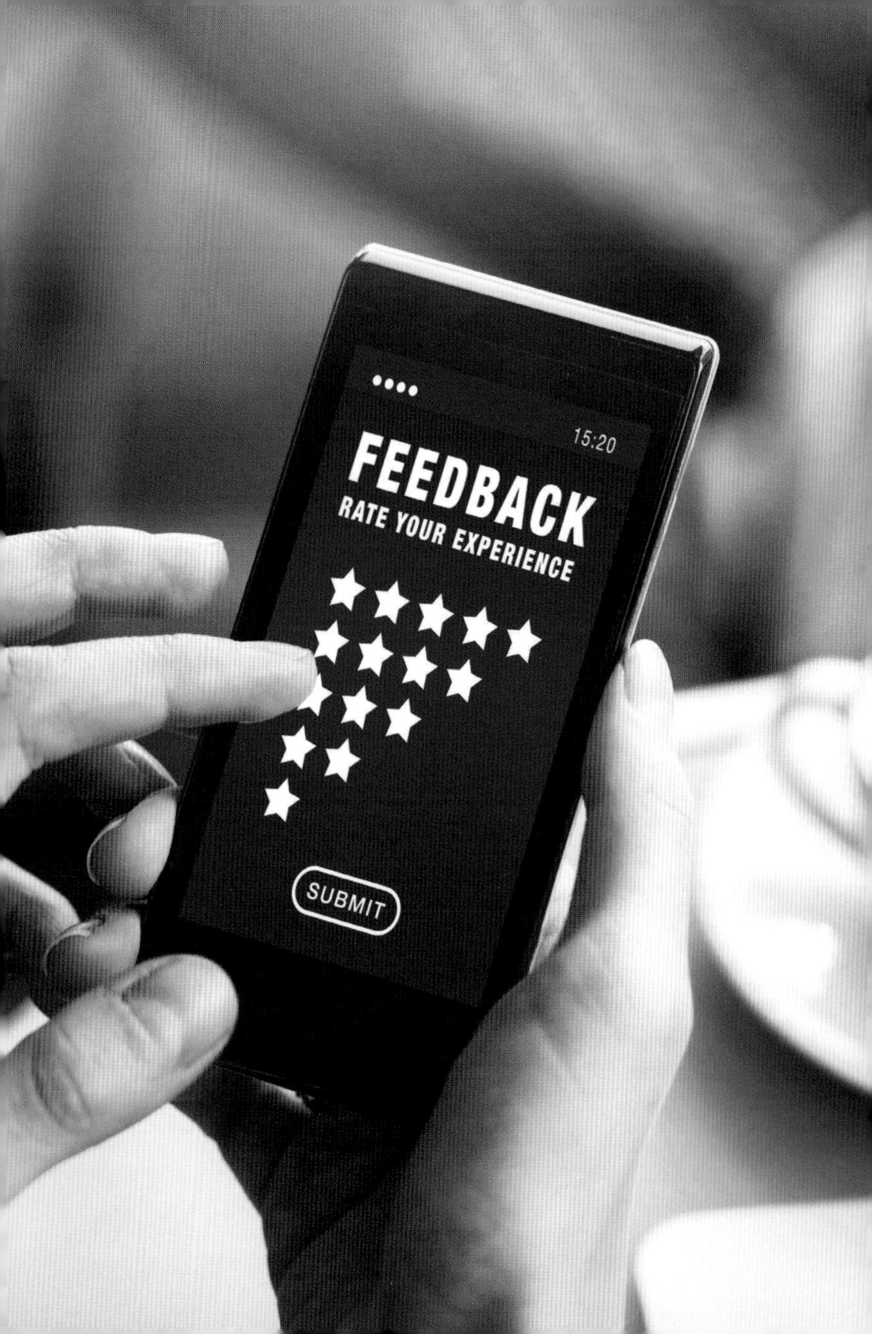
15:20
FEEDBACK
RATE YOUR EXPERIENCE
SUBMIT

evolution. Before the written word was developed, information was passed from generation to generation with stories. Our brains are wired for stories.

Many of us know from experience that great salespeople (and great executives) are great storytellers. The biggest generator of emotion is a customer story, especially when the buyer's brain can feel itself in the story. Near the end of the story, their brain creates a potentially similar story for them.

Many neuroscience laboratories have used functional MRIs to develop an optimum story architecture that will best wake up the buyer's decision-making brain. The best ones have six elements:

1 Start with the buyer's emotion about their challenge or objective.

2 Relate the story directly to the buyer.

3 Make the story personal about one of your current customers (i.e., use the customer's first name).

4 Include details to show that you really lived it with the customer.

5 Have a clear point about the result the customer received, such as the financial return your customer realized.

6 Finish with the customer's positive emotions (e.g., got a promotion because of your help).

In our new virtual world, there is now a fourth way to differentiate. Buyers expect your website to have great content so they can learn on their own. Buyers are also looking for expert help to accelerate their change journey. Therefore, the overall digital presence of your company has suddenly become very import-ant. B2B buyers complete 90 percent of their path to purchase before most companies even recognize them as a prospect. They will only reach out to the companies they are seriously considering near the end of their decision-making process.

To achieve this level of digital competence, companies need to be brilliant in the six pillars of digital dominance:

Pillar #1: Strategic Planning

Digital strength has to be focused on an overall digital marketing strategy. This digital strategy flows from the company's business strategy and then to the total marketing strategy that will likely still include substantial effort in traditional marketing. This is the step where you determine how much to invest in each pillar to achieve your business growth goals.

Domain authority is a key performance metric in getting your strategy right. It gauges whether your company's website is likely to show up in search results for particular keywords. If it does show up, on which page? Where on the page? And where does your company stand relative to the competition? In our personal lives, our domain authority score would be our credit rating.

Pillar #2: Convincing Information

Getting information to prospect about your company, products, and services is what digital marketing is all about; it tells your story in a convincing way. The bulk of information distribution to prospective clients is from your website, landing pages for singular purposes, or your social media posts in the form of blogs, posts, images, and videos.

Buyers expect to get almost all of their information before they ever reach out to somebody in your company. If you can't get your information out there on the internet, have it be easily understandable, and answer all buyer questions, then you will potentially lose business to your competitors.

A great website should be interactive, informative, and complete. It's not enough to just have a brochure-type website with limited information. The same is true for the social media sites you choose to work with.

How many pages of content do you have? How many backlinks? Do you use blog posts, photos, and video robustly? You need to utilize all aspects of your website and be knowledgeable about everything your buyers show you about the information they need to buy from you. Know how they buy and give them what they want on your website.

Pillar #3: Traffic Generation

You have to get eyes on your information from qualified leads. The more visitors you have to your website, landing pages, and social media sites, the more leads you will generate and the more sales you will make online. It's a numbers game and a focus game, getting more of the right kinds of visitors on your site, those that you can call prospects.

What are your SEO (search engine optimization) results? How many visitors per month do you get from organic search traffic and how many for ranked terms? How many of your pages are ranked on page one? Do you have a balance between late-stage branded traffic and early-stage nonbranded?

SEO, paid advertising (Google, LinkedIn, and Facebook advertising), and social media integration with your website are critical. There are other ways to generate traffic, but the basics are still SEO, paid ads, and social media.

Pillar #4: Analytics and Testing

Are you measuring useful activity and results from your website, SEO, advertising, and social media investments? There is a significant amount of free data available from Google Analytics, social media platforms, and automation tools. How are you measuring both leading indicators (traffic, downloads, calls) and lagging indicators (sales, appointments)?

With the proper use of analytics, a big part of success is constant testing. No digital marketing campaign will ever reach its full potential without measuring, testing, and measuring again. Companies like Amazon have perfected this with many tests gradually making huge improvements in performance.

Pillar #5: Lead Generation

A great website and tons of traffic are great, but you have to "convert" that traffic to leads and then sales for your digital investments to work. How you entice visitors to call you or download your virtual demo in exchange for their email address is critical.

This is the equivalent of "trial closing" in F2F sales. On each page and in each social media post, use a trial close to get the visitor to contact you *if* they are a qualified lead. Make it clear to visitors who are not good prospects for you that they are not in the right place.

Pillar #6: Nurturing and Closing

If your products or services have any sales cycle time at all, you will have to nurture the leads and convince them you are the right company from which to buy. Technology is playing a huge role with marketing automation tools and AI coming into its own in the sales process.

How is your company using email marketing, marketing automation, smartphone systems, and CRM? Don't forget that social media is critical in this nurturing and closing step of digital marketing.

After differentiating your offerings as appropriate and when the buyer is ready, it is time to propose a close. Closing usually takes two paths: either closing the sale now or, in some cases, such as for larger sales

and/or sales with longer sales cycle times, closing the next step in the buyer's buying process. Let's take closing the next step first.

Here is a bad example: "*Based on our discussion, Bob, I will send you a relevant video.*" Ho-hum.

It would be better if you added, "*Because I want you to see the tremendous benefit this solution will have on your operational efficiency.*"

And best if you continued, "*When you get the video, will you take a look and get back to me?*"

When the buyer says yes, you have closed the next step in the staircase to the final yes.

When you are ready to directly ask for the order, there are ten ways to do so. For each of the ten, there are two different situations: normal times and during a recession (e.g., the recent pandemic).

METHOD	NORMAL TIME	RECESSION
Extended terms (products)	30 days	90 days
Technology	Annual payment upfront	Monthly payment
Subscription model	Annual payment upfront after short trial period	First six months free on a three-year contract
Free trial access to software	15–30 days	Up to 90 days
Offer additional feature/ product free w/large purchases	No need	Yes
Offer newer, smaller in scope, and less expensive versions of large systems/ products	No need	Yes
Unbundle combined offerings and sell them separately	No need	Yes
Discount on first sale	No need	Yes
Bartering	Perhaps	Yes
Offer financing from the seller company or the seller's bank	No need	Yes

CHAPTER

SIX

Fundamental Tools Needed for Sales Success

To make sales, you need to have the right tools. There are many we recommend, and like the changing market, more are always coming. However, there are some fundamental tools (some specific applications, some application types) that make working in sales in our modern times far simpler. The following tools and programs can make a world of difference for you and your team's success.

CRM

Customer relationship management (CRM) tools are critical for salespeople who have a hunting responsibility. These tools enable salespeople to efficiently manage their current accounts and prospects. CRM capabilities include automatic reminders, analysis of pipeline stages, analysis of deals won and lost, and revenue reports.

Well-known vendors include Salesforce, Oracle, SAP, Microsoft Dynamics, NetSuite, HubSpot, and Sugar.

LinkedIn Essentials

LinkedIn is a 24/7/365 online networking event, the digital representation of your professional image. With that in mind, your profile should be customer facing, not job seeking. Some tips for the best customer response include the following:

- *Use a professional headshot to get four times more profile views and become thirty-six times more likely to receive a message.[xiv]*

- *Include videos of you speaking to a group, which give instant credibility.*

- *Always pay attention to the headers and footers in your profile. A background photo of a header should represent your brand and be consistent with website images (who you are).*

- *Your headline is the brief description appearing next to your name; it is equivalent to the subject line in an email. Write it so it conveys benefits to the viewer. It is important when buyers search for people like you. Use keywords tied to your services.*

- *You can go above and beyond by also putting videos showing your expertise in the Featured Section.*

The biggest tip for LinkedIn success is simple: be active on LinkedIn every day. Follow current clients, target accounts, and their competitor company pages.

Look for coaches (your business friends) for introductions. Share, like, and create content.

Sales Navigator

Elite salespeople are using Sales Navigator as a must-have tool for hunting salespeople. It provides higher level tools and shortcuts within the LinkedIn platform. Examples of the tools are as follows:

- *Advanced search to identify targeted companies*
- *Advanced search to ID prospects with additional filters for account based marketing (identifying potential qualified leads)*
- *Advanced search to map organization charts (to identify all buyers)*
- *Saved search ability to identify future prospects*
- *Technology to determine personality style (Crystal Knows plug-in)*

- *Team Link so multiple salespeople in the same company can collaborate*
- *Use of first-degree connections for introductions*
- *Unique visibility to third-degree connections that are five times more likely to connect*
- *Ability to connect using InMail to prospects outside your network*
- *News about people you have designated as Leads shows up in your Navigator News feed, making it easier to stay on top of the latest news about your prospects AND making it easier to get a conversation started*
- *Navigator "learns" what you are looking for in a lead, and suggests prospects similar to your filters, helping you discover prospects you might otherwise miss*
- *Ability to do the LinkedIn "dance" with targets at a high probability of connection as follows in the next section*

LinkedIn "Dance" with Sales Navigator

The best way to understand the possible applications of LinkedIn Sales Navigator is through cases of success. Here is one such an example of doing the LinkedIn "dance."

You meet somebody as part of a golf game or a group bike ride. Maybe you meet them at a virtual trade show or as part of a large company on a Zoom meeting. First, take a look at their LinkedIn profile. Then look at it again on day three and again on day five. If they look back at your profile, showing interest, ask them to connect. If not, send them an email with value to them, not about how great you are as described in Chapter 2. Give them a call. Don't be surprised if you get a voicemail. Be totally ready to leave a voicemail tuned to their personality style. By day eight, if they haven't looked at your profile, ask them to connect. Then, see what else is going on with them, and follow them on the social media platforms they're involved in. Respond to their posts by "liking" them and responding with a "thought leadership" post from your company or a branded third party source.. Then call them again. Keep this omnichannel prospecting process going using different sequences and different communication channels.

If you keep mixing it up, you're keeping the opportunity warm. You're increasing your mindshare in the buyer's mind.

Marketing Automation

Marketing automation (MA) refers to software platforms and technologies designed for marketing departments and organizations to more effectively market on multiple channels online, automate repetitive marketing tasks, and score leads that visit the company's website. MA also gives marketers the ability to create one-on-one cross-channel journeys that deliver a consistent, connected customer experience. One of its primary purposes is to deliver the right content at the right time to the right customers, in turn nurturing their trust in your brand.

MA platforms also contain lead scoring systems. The customer score increases depending on their title, their number of visits, and their activity on your website. An example would be if a visitor watches a video once, the MA might give that lead a score of five points. If the visitor watches the same video again, indicating great interest, the MA might add twenty more points.

The output of MA is marketing qualified leads for salespeople. MA can provide useful information for the salesperson who is following up on these leads. The salesperson can see which videos the lead watched, which blogs they read, and which ebooks they downloaded, indicating the lead's areas of interest.

Well-known vendors include SharpSpring, Act-On, HubSpot, Infusionsoft, Marketo, and Salesforce's Pardot.

Crystal Knows

Crystal Knows (CK) is a software platform that predicts people's personality types based on their DISC profile and their activities on social media platforms.

Based on the profile, CK will draft an email or voicemail based on the lead's personality style. CK will also show you how to deal with the prospect in person or on a video meetup.

The main benefit is that it allows salespeople to be able to match (same personality type) or mirror (different personality type) the buyer. Many salespeople are very good at selling to buyers who have their same personality type but do not do well selling to buyers with the other three personality types (see Chapter 3).

Here is an example of CK's use. Our team was drafting a presentation to a prospect of a large business. The marketing and sales team drafting the proposal showed their presentation to our VP of sales. It was twenty-five slides with lots of detail.

She asked the group about the personality style of

the economic buyer, the final decision maker. No one knew. She quickly went to CK and discovered that the buyer was a "Dominant" type (from the D in DISC). She deleted the proposal and asked the team to start over and come back with five big picture slides including a case study with return on investment. Based on that change, she closed the deal. A picture-perfect example of the value of CK.

Check out Crystal Knows at www.crystalknows .com.

Vocal Analytics

Our vocal profiles (how we sound to others) have increased in importance in a virtual sales world. A large study at UCLA by Dr. Albert Mehrabian found that the decision-making brain makes a first impression of another person based on what we see (55 percent), how they sound (38 percent), and what they actually say (7 percent). On the phone (no visual), these percentages change to 82 percent for how they sound and 18 percent for what they actually say. So the importance of your vocal profile is pretty obvious.

A new technology, an audio analytics engine called VoiceVibes, has built a large proprietary data set to measure human perception of voice to determine what "vibe" a typical audience would get from you. VoiceVibes is an AI-powered practice and coaching platform that helps people sound more natural and polished when they speak so they can transform how others perceive them.

VoiceVibes was acquired by Bigtincan early in 2021. Learn more about this AI-enabled speech coaching software at myvoicevibes.com and bigtincan.com.

Mobile Apps

As discussed in Chapter 1, mobile app use for buying products is rapidly increasing. Most buyers surveyed said they would increase their use of self-service options, including mobile apps, in the future. Companies cannot fall behind and let their competitors overtake them.

Subscription Business Models

In her new book, *The Forever Transaction: How to Build a Subscription Model So Compelling, Your Customers Will Never Want to Leave*, Robbie Kellman Baxter claims that every company can have a subscription business model. Her book has the recipe for developing one.

There is a reason private equity firms value companies selling via this model four to six times more than companies without it. The recurring revenue is the factor that enables such a high evaluation.

Automated Demos

Salespeople have been providing demos to buyers for decades. A demo can increase the buyer's knowledge

of the technology and increase their confidence that they are making the right buying decision.

Many buyers would now like to be able to see an automated demo that is faster, shorter, and to the point. Others still want a demo with a sales rep, and still others want to combine the two, watching an automated demo with the sales rep in attendance.

E-Commerce

We have all seen the rapid digitization of the economy. According to an article in the May/June 2020 edition of the *Harvard Business Review*, a third of companies selling B2B had a digital strategy coming into the 2020 pandemic.[xv] *Harvard Business Review* predicts that two-thirds of these companies will need one as the economy fully recovers.

All B2B companies need to make it easy and secure for customers and prospects to buy products and services online. We cannot let our competitors implement a brilliant e-commerce strategy and expect to survive without one.

AI Tools

A number of the tools for salespeople, such as CRM, Crystal Knows, Sales Navigator, and VoiceVibes, have AI tools embedded in them, but there are many stand-alone AI tools as well. Top sales reps spend twice as much time using AI tools than lower performing reps do. These tools have five principal capabilities:

1. Identifying strong prospects more efficiently using multichannel prospecting systems

2. Identifying the sales rep's next logical step with a prospect by analyzing buyer signals

3. Identifying which sales rep behaviors and channels help most to win sales by analyzing completed

deals (something only large companies have thus far been able to do)

4 Price optimization to get optimum combination of revenue and gross margin

5 Territory optimization

Sales Leadership in the Digital Sales Arena

Sales leaders are facing a dizzying array of digital tool options and streams of data. The challenge is to find out what works best for you and your sales teams. For example, monitoring sales rep communications. AI applications can give sales leaders finely detailed analytics on sales rep emails, phone calls, texts, and chats.[xvi] This data can be very helpful, but it's not a substitute for human involvement in managing sales teams. According to our studies of hundreds of sales managers, when they regularly and personally listen in to sales rep calls to prospects and current customers, they get an average 36 percent lift in win rate. In our company, we have reps periodically listening into calls by other reps and offering advice and encouragement, to the great benefit of the whole team.

Tools are only as good as you employ them. Sales leaders should embrace the concept of digital sales and be on the lookout for new technologies, but remind themselves that leadership cannot be digitized.

CHAPTER

SEVEN

Summing It All Up

What does the growth of digital capabilities mean for the future sales environment? What kind of salespeople will be needed five years from now? What skills will they need? Will F2F sales even be a profession?

Here are my predictions:

▸ *All companies will need to develop a written-down digital strategy:*

- A transformation in sales strategy, processes, and resource allocation is needed from seller-centric to buyer-centric, from analog to hyper-automated, from F2F to digital, and from modest to robust technology investment.

- Companies will need to build digital sales experiences to support customers' self-learning to qualify themselves and their understanding of their change journey to your company

- Savings can be significant in travel and commuting costs, office space, lower cost of living areas, and reduced carbon footprint

▸ *There will always be a need for salespeople because we are social beings. Interactions between buyer and seller will always be necessary to establish rapport and trust.*

▸ *For large, complicated, and technical sales, high-level salespeople will still be required. They will need a moderately high IQ, high EQ (emotional intelligence), technological know-how, high sales aptitude, and* be comfortable selling at the "C" level. They will also need a tireless work ethic, excellent writing capability, self-motivation, independent decision-making, and neuroscience-based sales skills.

▸ By 2025, 80 percent of interactions buyers will have salespeople and their companies will be digital. In most cases, the first interaction will be digital. Salespeople will need expertise with technology tools: CRM, LinkedIn/Sales Navigator, Crystal Knows (or equivalent), video conferencing platforms, AI tools, "voice vibe" evaluation, work collaboration platforms, PowerPoint, Google Analytics, and marketing automation.

▸ Today, the beginning third of the sales process is already being performed by marketing using automated tools that deliver qualified leads to salespeople, and this trend will continue. Time-consuming prospecting for new leads by salespeople will no longer be necessary.

▸ Many sales will occur without the need for a sales

rep, using technology such as automated demos, mobile apps for purchasing, virtual and augmented reality tools, subscription models, and e-commerce platforms with interactive portals.

▶ *AI tools will handle many routine sales and marketing tasks, obviating the need for as many people in sales positions, such as customer service reps and lead generation specialists.*

If you and your company are going to thrive and prosper, you need to acknowledge that the future of sales has a growing and dynamic digital component. There already are radical and permanent changes in buyer behavior. Traditional social selling techniques, such as building rapport and trust, performing a needs analysis, offering a compelling solution, and closing sales, are still essential to the sales process but need to be aligned with new digital technologies.

If you are a future salesperson, you will need to be a subject matter expert and demonstrate high levels of expertise in both technical systems and human systems. If you are a future sales leader, you will need to think through and devise a digital strategy and invest in your company's digital presence and selling systems. It all sounds daunting, but wasn't it just a few years ago that salespeople's lives became so much better with a cell phone and computer rather than a desk phone and a phone book? Sales is the same. We can keep improving the game.

Notes

i   Ethan Cramer-Flood, "Global Ecommerce Update 2021," eMarketer, January 13, 2021, https://www.emarketer.com/content /global-ecommerce-update-2021.

ii   "Digital Advertising Spending Worldwide from 2017 to 2024, by Format," Statista, July 2020, https://www.statista.com/stat istics/456679/digital-advertising-revenue-format-digital-market -outlook-worldwide/.

iii   Jaana Remes, et al., "Solving the Productivity Puzzle: The Role of Demand and the Promise of Digitization," McKinsey Global Institute (February 2018): 105, https://www.mckinsey.com /~/media/mckinsey/featured%20insights/meeting%20societys %20expectations/solving%20the%20productivity%20puzzle /mg-solving-the-productivity-puzzle--report-february-2018.pdf.

iv   Shelley E. Kohan, "Fueled by Increased Consumer Comfort, Mobile Payments in the U.S. Will Exceed $130 Billion in 2020," *Forbes*, March 1, 2020, https://www.forbes.com/sites/shelley

kohan/2020/03/01/fueled-by-increased-consumer-comfort-mobile -payments-in-the-uswill-exceed-130-billion-in-2020/?sh=4c19 fdf744f2.

v   Beatriz Estay, "16 Online Shopping Statistics: How Many People Shop Online?" BigCommerce, https://www.bigcommerce.com /blog/online-shopping-statistics/#5-essential-online-shopping -statistics.

vi   "The LinkedIn State of Sales Report 2020," LinkedIn Sales Solutions, https://business.linkedin.com/sales-solutions/b2b-sales -strategy-guides/the-state-of-sales-2020-report.

vii   Kelly Blum, "Gartner Says 80% of B2B Sales Interactions Between Suppliers and Buyers Will Occur in Digital Channels by 2025," Gartner Press Release, September 15, 2020, https://www.gartner .com/en/newsroom/press-releases/2020-09-15-gartner-says-80 --of-b2b-sales-interactions-between-su.

viii   "The LinkedIn State of Sales Report 2020," LinkedIn Sales Solutions, https://business.linkedin.com/sales-solutions/b2b-sales -strategy-guides/the-state-of-sales-2020-report.

ix   "PwC's US Remote Work Survey: It's Time to Reimagine Where and How Work Will Get Done," PwC, January 12, 2021, https:// www.pwc.com/us/en/library/covid-19/us-remote-work-survey.html.

x   Mary Shea, PhD, et al., "The Democratization of B2B Sales," Forrester Research, August 3, 2020, https://www.forrester.com /report/The+Democratization+Of+B2B+Sales/-/E-RES149555.

xi   Michael Gentle, "How Millennials Are Changing the B2B Buyer Profile," Branding Strategy Insider, June 12, 2019, https://www

.brandingstrategyinsider.com/how-millennials-are-changing-the -b2b-buyer-profile/#.YBWq7C1h2IE.

xii   Alex Hisaka, "How B2B Buyers Perceive Sales Professionals," LinkedIn Sales Blog, September 16, 2014, https://www.linkedin .com/business/sales/blog/guides/how-b2b-buyers-perceive-sales -professionals.

xiii   Matthew Croghan, "Top 50 LinkedIn Stats That You Need to Know for Lead Generation," Linked Selling, accessed February 25, 2021, https://linkedselling.com/linkedin-stats-for-lead-gen.

xiv   Meero Team, "11 Tips to Follow for the Perfect LinkedIn Profile Picture in 2020," Meero.com, July 16, 2020, https://www.meero .com/en/news/corporate/411/11-Tips-To-Follow-For-The-Perfect -Linkedin-Profile-Picture-In-2019.

xv   Rita Gunther McGrath and Ryan McManus, "Discovery-Driven Digital Transformation," *Harvard Business Review*, May–June 2020, https://hbr.org/2020/05/discovery-driven-digital-trans formation.

xvi   Cem Dilmegani, "AI in Sales: 15 AI Sales Applications/Use Cases in 2021," AIMultiple, January 5, 2021, https://research.aimultiple .com/sales-ai/.

Acknowledgments

I would like to acknowledge the many outstanding associates in our company who had a significant impact behind the tools, tips, and techniques in the manuscript. I am grateful for their knowledge and expertise.

Steve Johnson is a Vistage Chair who has heard over one hundred great speakers, many of whom spoke on sales. His overall knowledge of the sales industry was instrumental in keeping the book grounded and accurate. In addition, Steve is an expert on leadership and management. As we all know, the great leaders and managers are great storytellers and therefore elite salespeople. Steve is one of those!

Debra Borchardt is a world-class editor who made

sure our spelling, grammar, and use of just the right words was always on the mark.

Dr. Dave Potts was my alter ego as a great researcher and ghost author. Dave has been in government acquisition, government sales, and international business development. He is the author of *Customer Relations and Sales from A to Z* and coauthor of *Etiquette for Engineers.*

Kim Bialozynski has a rock-solid background in sales, management, marketing, and marketing integration. She kept us grounded in the pre- and post-pandemic realties. Kim kept in close contact with our clients throughout the pandemic and maintained great relationships. She also created many new ones.

Kyla O'Connell and I have collaborated on many projects for over ten years in the company. She lent her vast experience as a sales trainer and master sales coach. She is very forward focused and helped develop many ideas to keep our team motivated and engaged.

Amy Sawyer kept us all on track and in line. She is

the epitome of a "team player." She is there for all of us, all the time.

Thanks to all of our business partners, especially Fred Diamond of the Institute for Excellence in Sales, John Edwards at Communica, Hube Hopkins at WSI B2B Marketing, and Judy Schramm at ProResource.

Thanks to everyone for exceptional input and support. It truly does take a village, and the Asher team is brilliant in all of these areas.

In many ways, this book is an integration of research surveys and studies of outstanding companies who freely shared their research to their subscribers. These include:

- *The Wharton School of the University of Pennsylvania*
- *McKinsey & Company*
- *Harvard Business Review*
- *ringDNA*
- *LinkedIn*
- *Vistage International*
- *Gartner*

- *Wall Street Journal*
- *McKinsey Daily Read*
- *FCW Insider*
- *Forrester*
- *Selling Power*
- *Sandler*
- *ASLAN Sales*
- *TED Talks Daily*

Finally, my partner and wife, Debb Borchardt, receives a double thank you for the endless nights we missed together while I was focusing on the book. Thank you, Debb!

About the Author

In his first career, John Asher was captain of two nuclear-powered fast attack submarines. In his final job in the U.S. Navy, he was the program manager of a billion-dollar software development program. A lot of what he learned about leadership and sales he learned in the U.S. Navy.

In John's second career, he cofounded an engineering company that grew at a rate of 42 percent year over year, which compounded for fourteen straight years. Along the way, the firm acquired seven other companies, and John gained key insights into what it takes to develop a fast-growing business where everybody in the company is in sales!

In his third career, John started a sales and marketing advisory business to share the lessons he learned from being on the front lines of selling complex products and services for over twenty years. Those lessons were translated into his top ten selling skills that are the blocking and tackling of successful sales. He and his team have trained over seventy thousand salespeople in twenty-two countries on his efficient and effective sales process to quickly close new business.

Over the last two decades, John has mentored a large cadre of speakers and trainers that has fueled the growth of ASHER.

In 2015, he received the Lifetime Speaker Achievement Award for extraordinary contributions to Vistage, an international organization of CEOs. In

2020, he also received the Vistage Club 1000 Award. John was named "2021 Member of the Year" by the Institute for Excellence in Sales.

In 2018, John and five others including Dr. Jeffrey Boone, world renowned cardiologist, founded the Asher Longevity Institute with the mission of helping others live better and longer lives.

John's first book was published in China in Mandarin in 2013. It was a sales book teaching Chinese salespeople how to sell to Western companies, and was funded by Alibaba and Haier. His second book, *Close Deals Faster*, is an award winner in the business sales category of the 2018 International Book Awards. His third-book, *The Neuroscience of Selling: Proven Sales Secrets to Win Over the Buyer's Heart and Mind*, sold out when first available on Amazon.

NEW! Only from Simple Truths®

IGNITE READS
spark impact in just one hour

IGNITE READS IS A NEW SERIES OF 1-HOUR READS WRITTEN BY WORLD-RENOWNED EXPERTS!

These captivating books will help you become the best version of yourself, allowing for new opportunities in your personal and professional life. Accelerate your career and expand your knowledge with these powerful books written on today's hottest ideas.

TRENDING BUSINESS AND PERSONAL GROWTH TOPICS

 Read in an hour or less

 Leading experts and authors

 Bold design and captivating content